WORLD WAR II

GENERALS OF WORLD WAR II

Mike Taylor

Visit us at
www.abdopub.com

Published by Abdo Publishing Company, 4940 Viking Drive, Edina, MN 55435.

Printed in the United States.

Interior Graphic Design: John Hamilton
Cover Design: MacLean & Tuminelly
Contributing Editors: John Hamilton; Morgan Hughes
Cover photo: Digital Stock
Interior photos: Digital Stock, pages 1, 3, 4, 5, 17, 18, 19, 22, 23, 27, 28, 31
Corbis, pages 6, 8, 11, 13, 14, 16, 18, 19, 21, 24

Sources: Churchill, Winston S. *The Second World War.* 6 vols. New York, 1948-1953. Stokesbury, James L. *A Short History of World War II.* William Morrow and Company, 1980. Weinberg, Gerhard. *A World At Arms, a Global History of World War II.* Cambridge University Press, 1994.Wright, Gordon. *The Ordeal of Total War, 1939-1945.* Harper & Row, 1968. Young, Desmond. *Rommel: The Desert Fox.* Harpers & Brothers, 1950.

Library of Congress Cataloging–in–Publication Data

Taylor, Mike, 1965-
    Generals of World War II / Mike Taylor
        p. cm. — (World War II)
    Includes index.
    Summary: An account of the battlefield activities of German, British, American, and Russian generals during the largest war in history.
    ISBN   1-56239-805-9 (alk. paper)
    1. World War, 1939-1945—Biography—Juvenile literature. 2. Generals— Biography—Juvenile literature. [1. World War, 1939-1945—Biography.
 2. Generals.] I. Title. II. Series: World War II (Edina, Minn.)
D736.T357   1998
940.53'092—dc21   98-6473
[b]   CIP
                                                              AC

CONTENTS

Anti-tank infantrymen scurry for cover.

THE WORLD AT WAR

General Douglas MacArthur lands at Leyte, Philippines.

World War II began in 1939 when Germany invaded Poland. Germany was led by the dictator Adolf Hitler, who hoped to use Germany's powerful army to conquer all of Europe. Other countries in Europe, especially France and Great Britain, rallied to stop Hitler.

On the other side of the world, Germany had a powerful ally in Japan. Japan hoped to conquer the islands of the South Pacific, and believed it was necessary to defeat the United States in order to realize that goal. Japan attacked the United States at Pearl Harbor on December 7, 1941. Germany, Italy, and Japan together were called the Axis powers.

After the Japanese surprise attack on Pearl Harbor, the United States joined the fight against the Axis powers. The Soviet Union soon fought against the

Axis powers also. The United States, Great Britain, and the Soviet Union together were called the Allies. (The Allies also included many other less-powerful countries joined together to fight the Axis powers.)

The Allies finally defeated the Axis powers during the summer of 1945, almost six years after the war began. Germany's powerful army fought very well, nearly winning the war during the first year. In the end, however, Adolf Hitler's military decisions proved wrong, and the great Allied armies crushed Germany from the east and from the west. Without support from Germany, Japan could not fight for long and surrendered a few months later.

A U.S. Marine dashes through Death Valley on Okinawa.

HITLER'S GENERALS

Adolf Hitler congratulating General Fedor von Bock.

When the war began, Germany had the world's most powerful army. It was well trained and possessed outstanding weapons, including excellent tanks and aircraft. German generals had developed a new strategy called *Blitzkrieg* (lightning warfare) to use these weapons in the conquest of Europe.

Hitler's generals attacked Poland in August 1939 with two armies, one from the north and one from the south. The northern army was commanded by General Fedor von Bock. The southern army was led by General Gerd von Runstedt. Bock and Runstedt tried to push east from Germany, then circle and meet deep in Poland, surrounding the Polish army.

Bock and Runstedt were masters of the *Blitzkrieg* style of warfare. They used speedy tanks to punch holes in the Polish lines of defense. Meanwhile, their dive bombers and other planes attacked railroads and highways to prevent the Polish army from moving to patch the holes. Then German foot soldiers poured through the holes to capture Polish weapons and supplies, especially fuel for tanks, trucks, and planes. After just two weeks of fighting, the Polish army was surrounded and forced to surrender.

The world was shocked as the Germans turned the *Blitzkrieg* against its neighbors to the north, Denmark and Norway. During the winter of 1939 and 1940 it seemed that the German army would indeed use *Blitzkrieg* to overrun Europe as quickly as lightning.

After defeating Poland, Denmark, and Norway, Hitler's great tank commanders turned their attention to France, Germany's neighbor to the west. France had constructed a huge line of defense known as the "Maginot Line." Named after the French general who had invented the plan, the Maginot Line was a long chain of fortresses in eastern France constructed to defend against a German invasion. The fortresses in the Maginot Line were connected by long underground railways to transport troops quickly and safely from place to place. In this way, General Maginot hoped, France could respond quickly and fill any holes that the Germans managed to punch through their line of defense.

The Maginot Line extended all the way from Switzerland in the south to the Ardennes Forest in the north. Maginot knew that the German army could never cross through the high mountains of

Switzerland to get around the south end of the Maginot Line. He also believed that the Germans could not pass through the rugged Ardennes Forest to get around the north end of the Maginot Line. The French nation believed it was safe behind the Maginot Line and waited with confidence for the German attack.

Hitler was not sure that *Blitzkrieg* would work against France. He knew that the German army could not penetrate the Maginot Line, and feared it would have to go around the line to the north. It would be dangerous to drive tanks and trucks through the thick trees and rugged terrain of the Ardennes Forest.

Nonetheless, skilled tank commanders, like Generals Heinz Guderian and Erwin Rommel, were confident that *Blitzkrieg* would work in France just as it had worked in Poland. They reassured Hitler that their tanks could indeed pass through the Ardennes

General Runstedt walks between Adolf Hitler and Benito Mussolini as they tour a battle site on the Eastern Front.

Forest. Hitler trusted the judgement of his generals in this matter and agreed to their plan.

On May 10, 1940, a diversion attack was launched far to the north, along the sea coast through Belgium. France, believing that the attack in Belgium was the main German attack, rushed most of its army there to stop the invasion. Great Britain came to the assistance of its ally and sent its army to fight with France in Belgium.

As the French and British fought for their lives in Belgium, the tanks of Guderian and Rommel crept carefully through the wilds of the Ardennes Forest. Within a few days the German army was through the Ardennes Forest and drove quickly across France. The French suddenly realized their mistake. The great Maginot Line was now useless because the Germans had accomplished the impossible: they had passed through the Ardennes Forest.

The French had sent almost all their troops to the battle in Belgium. This left almost no weapons to stop Rommel and Guderian. With amazing speed, Rommel and Guderian drove across France to surround the British and the French to the north. By May 26 Rommel and Guderian surrounded the French and British armies in the town of Dunkirk, a small port in northern France.

Fearing the capture of its entire army, the British government ordered every ship in the area to speed to Dunkirk. In what was called the "Miracle of Dunkirk," hundreds of British ships, including cargo ships and

9

even fishing boats, managed to rescue the British and French armies from Dunkirk. (Germany hesitated in assaulting Dunkirk, partly because of Hitler's unwillingness to risk armor.) Before the tanks of Generals Rommel and Guderian could move in, the British army escaped.

Germany's tank commanders won the Battle of France, despite the "Miracle of Dunkirk." France surrendered in June 1940. While General Guderian remained in Europe to fight close to home, Hitler transferred General Rommel to North Africa to fight the British there.

Rommel's army controlled much of North Africa. Rommel hoped to defeat British troops in Egypt and conquer the country for Germany. During 1941 and 1942 Rommel enjoyed great success against the British. Because of his skill and cunning in desert-style tank warfare, Rommel earned the nickname, "Desert Fox."

Upon arrival in North Africa, Rommel worried first that the British would learn how weak and outnumbered Germany's forces really were. This would give Great Britain the advantage because they would know to attack with full confidence over the weaker German force. In order to hide the weakness of his army from British spy planes, Rommel used canvas to disguise cars, trucks, and even desert boulders so that they looked like German tanks. In the meanwhile, Rommel transported real tanks as quickly as possible from Germany.

German Field Marshal Erwin Rommel, the "Desert Fox."

By 1942 the Germans were prepared for an all-out attack on the British. Between January and June 1942 Rommel pushed the British army all the way across the Sahara Desert to the Egyptian border. Hitler was so pleased that he promoted Rommel to the rank of field marshal, the highest ranking general in the German army.

While the "Desert Fox" was winning battle after battle in North Africa, Germany's forces in Europe invaded the Soviet Union. It was here that Hitler showed his poorest leadership and made his worst mistakes of the war.

Things went well for the Germans at first, and by the middle of 1942 they had conquered a huge amount of territory in the western Soviet Union. At the end of 1942, however, things began to go badly.

The German Fourth Army, led by General Friedrich von Paulus, attempted to capture the Soviet city of Stalingrad. Soviet troops fought heroically in one of the most brutal battles of the entire war. The weather was cold and the Germans ran low on food, ammunition, and fuel.

Paulus asked Hitler for permission to call off the attack and reorganize, but Hitler would not allow it. Instead, Hitler ordered Paulus to fight to the death. The result was horrible. Stranded German soldiers starved and froze. Well over 200,000 German soldiers perished in the fighting.

Finally, ignoring Hitler's orders, Paulus surrendered to the Soviet army on January 31, 1943 (the very day Hitler promoted Paulus to field marshal, the highest rank in the German army). The Soviet Union took the surviving German troops as prisoners. Hitler was furious and denounced General Paulus as a traitor. (Hitler was distrustful of most of his generals, Paulus among them but by no means alone.)

Gradually, the German generals began to mistrust and dislike Hitler. Many of them thought Paulus should have retreated earlier to avoid capture. Hitler sensed the mistrust of his generals and began to ignore their expert advice. This was a mistake and gradually, after the Battle of Stalingrad, the Soviet Union began to win more and more battles against Germany.

German Field Marshal Friedrich von Paulus, shortly after being captured by the Soviets at Stalingrad.

THE BRITISH GENERALS

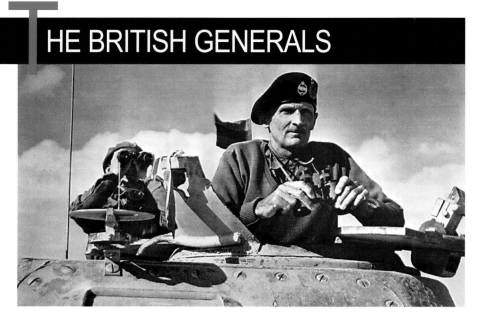

British Field Marshal Sir Bernard Law Montgomery surveys his troops from atop a British tank.

Rommel, the "Desert Fox," had bested two of Great Britain's top-ranking generals in 1941 and 1942. The first British commander in North Africa was Sir Archibald Wavell. He was dismissed in June 1941, and was replaced by General Claude Auchinleck, who managed some success against the "Desert Fox," pushing the German army back to the west.

Rommel earned a favorable reputation even among the British soldiers during this time. While they shot to kill each other in battle, German and British soldiers often shared fuel and water with one another in emergencies. Rommel's style of warfare was more humane than his leader, Adolf Hitler.

Rommel finally defeated Auchinleck, pushing almost as far as the Egyptian town of El Alamein. The Germans were now in Egypt, one of the crown jewels in the British Empire!

The British dismissed Auchinleck and replaced him with the team of Sir Harold Alexander and

Bernard Montgomery. General Alexander became the commander of all British forces in the area, while General Montgomery was Alexander's most successful field commander.

Like Rommel, General Montgomery was a very skilled tank commander and quickly learned the tactics of desert warfare. It was Montgomery who organized the British defense of El Alamein in 1942.

Montgomery's spies had broken the German code. Montgomery knew Rommel's every move in advance. To the amazement of his troops, "Monty" picked the exact time and place of Rommel's attack on El Alamein. British tanks and aircraft were lying in wait when Rommel attacked on August 30, 1942.

North Africa

Rommel's attack failed miserably. The British counter-attack began on October 23. (Rommel was absent from the area on sick leave. The "Desert Fox" returned two days later because his replacement, General Stumme, died of a heart attack during the attack.) Eight hundred British cannons bombarded Rommel's men for two days. Rommel now begged for permission to retreat, but Adolf Hitler wouldn't allow it, insisting again that the Germans fight to the end. Five days later, Montgomery retook El Alamein.

Finally, on November 5, 1942, the "Desert Fox" admitted defeat and fled westward, his army exhausted and short of ammunition. They had to abandon trucks and tanks as they fled because they had no more fuel.

THE AMERICAN GENERALS

Just as General Montgomery pushed the Germans from the east side of the Sahara Desert, a huge American and British invasion pushed the Germans from the west. "Operation Torch," the code name for the American invasion, took place in November 1942. American General Dwight D. Eisenhower was named as the supreme commander of the invasion, along with British Admiral John Cunningham. Eisenhower planned to trap the German army between his own army and the British army of General Montgomery, which was pushing from the east.

Although Eisenhower's plan worked very well, there was very heavy fighting. American and British troops came under heavy attack from Rommel and his German forces at the Battle of Kasserine Pass, in Tunisia.

The Germans were now cornered by the Americans to the west and the British to the east. In desperation, the Germans attacked through Kasserine Pass on February 14, 1943. In a few days the Germans killed 6,000 American

American Brigadier General Omar Bradley.

troops and lost only 1,000 of their own.

The disaster at Kasserine Pass was an embarrassment for General Eisenhower and the Americans. The British generals, Montgomery and Alexander, criticized the American leadership. Finally, General Eisenhower fired the American commander responsible for the disaster, replacing him with General George S. Patton and his deputy, General Omar Bradley.

American General Dwight D. "Ike" Eisenhower.

The American army learned quickly and had better success after the Battle of Kasserine Pass. Patton's army joined with Montgomery's and pushed the Germans out of North Africa completely in May 1943. Together, the British and Americans invaded Italy during the summer of 1943.

During the invasion of Italy, Generals Montgomery and Patton argued bitterly about tactics. Patton refused to cooperate with the British. He insisted on a completely American command of the invasion. Montgomery insisted on a British command. Despite the arguments between the Americans and the British, the two Allies worked well enough together to ensure victory over the Germans in Italy in 1943.

TIMELINE OF WORLD WAR II

1939 *September*: Battle of Poland. German *Blitzkrieg* overwhelms Poland with high-speed tanks and aircraft. The Battle of Poland was the beginning of World War II.

November 1939—May 1940: The Phony War. Britain and France declare war on Germany, but the fight doesn't start until May 1940.

1940 *August—September:* Battle of Britain. Britain uses newly invented radar units and fighter airplanes to intercept German bombers. The Battle of Britain was the largest air battle in World War II.

1941 *December 7:* Surprise attack on Pearl Harbor. Japanese aircraft carriers stage successful surprise attack and destroy much of the American fleet at Pearl Harbor in Hawaii. Because the Japanese used strict radio silence, it was impossible for the Americans to intercept messages and predict the attack.

1942 *June:* Battle of Midway. One of the greatest battles among aircraft carriers. Japanese aircraft carriers attack, but the Americans are prepared and win the battle decisively. The Americans sink four Japanese aircraft carriers. The Japanese sink one American carrier, the *Yorktown*.

1942 *August 7:* Battle of Guadalcanal. U.S. Marines use landing craft to invade and capture this important island from the Japanese.

1942-43 *Winter:* Battle of Stalingrad. Germans and Soviets engage in street-to-street and building-to-building battle for the Soviet city of Stalingrad. Small machine guns were very important to this style of fighting. In February 1943 the surviving Germans ran out of ammunition and supplies and were forced to surrender. German and Russian casualties totalled nearly 500,000 men.

1944 *June 6:* D-Day. Allied forces use hundreds of small landing craft to attack the beaches of northern France. The Allies landed so many soldiers in this way that they eventually liberated Paris and pushed the Germans out of France.

1945 *May 8:* V-E Day. Victory in Europe! The Germans surrender to American General Dwight D. Eisenhower.

1945 *August 6:* Hiroshima. American bomber *Enola Gay* drops an atomic bomb on the Japanese city of Hiroshima. Around 130,000 Japanese civilians are killed or injured. Three days later, on August 9, another atomic bomb is dropped on the city of Nagasaki.

1945 *August 14:* Japanese surrender. Japan surrenders to the Allies after witnessing the terrible destruction in the cities of Hiroshima and Nagasaki. The surrender documents are signed by Japanese representatives aboard the USS *Missouri*.

THE SOVIET GENERALS

While the British and Americans fought their way through Italy, the Soviet Union was having success against Germany as well. The army of the Soviet Union was a shambles until 1943. During the 1930s, before the war began, the Soviet government accused most of its generals of treason. The Soviet leader, Josef Stalin, feared these powerful men and insisted that they be executed. The result was that the Soviet Union lost its best generals before the war even began!

The disorganized Soviet army was beaten badly by Germany early in the war. The strategy of the Soviet generals was to retreat slowly, giving territory to the Germans, but making them pay a high price in blood.

The Battle of Stalingrad, in January 1943, was the turning point. The Soviet army defeated the Germans and captured General Friedrich von Paulus. By this time a new generation of Soviet generals replaced those killed during the 1930s. General Andrei Eremenko commanded all Soviet troops in the Stalingrad area, while General Vassily Chuikov commanded the troops located in the city.

Several times the Germans were within a few city blocks of Chuikov's headquarters. Chuikov's men retrenched heroically and fought the Germans off with close-range gun fire. Eremenko and Chuikov both became heroes when the Soviet army captured General Paulus and won the Battle of Stalingrad.

During the summer of 1943 Stalin planned a major attack on the German army in the prairies surrounding the city of Kursk. The Battle of Kursk was the largest tank battle in history, with each side using thousands of tanks. By this time the Germans were very low on fuel. Skilled Soviet tank commanders lured the enemy into the Kursk area and then surprised them with huge numbers of tanks and anti-tank guns.

Most famous of Josef Stalin's tank commanders in the Battle of Kursk was General Constantine Rokassovsky. After the Soviet victory in the Battle of Kursk, Rokassovsky became a hero around the world. In two weeks he had destroyed half of all of Germany's tanks!

Josef Stalin once again became fearful of the growing power of his generals. He was careful not to allow one general, like Rokassovsky, to win too many victories. In 1945 Stalin pretended to give Rokassovsky the honor of capturing the German capital of Berlin, but gave the honor to his trusted friend Marshal Georgi Zhukov instead at the last minute.

Soviet General Vasili Chuikov.

VICTORY OVER THE AXIS POWERS

An American soldier with German prisoners.

Because General Eisenhower had planned the successful invasion of North Africa, he was now called to plan the invasion of France as well. The invasion force would include nearly 200,000 men, British and Americans fighting side by side.

Most thought that Eisenhower would name General George Patton to command the invasion force. But Eisenhower agreed that since General Patton could not get along with the British, he would not command the invasion force. Instead, Patton's former deputy, General Omar Bradley, would command the American invasion force. This was a very impressive promotion for Bradley and great disappointment for Patton, his former boss!

General Bradley cooperated much more readily with the British and found a trusted comrade in British General Bernard Montgomery. It was Montgomery who had defeated Rommel, the "Desert Fox," in the Battle of El Alamein in 1942. While Montgomery commanded the British half of the invasion force, Bradley commanded the Americans.

The great D-Day invasion began on June 6, 1944. As these Allied armies landed in small boats on the beaches of Normandy, in northern France, it was none other than General Rommel himself who organized the German defenses.

In words that have since become famous, Rommel predicted that the first day of the battle would be "the longest day." By this, he meant that Germany needed to put all its troops on the invasion beaches to stop the Americans and British on the first day. If they did not do that, he predicted, Germany could not win the war.

Luckily for the Allies, Rommel was no longer the favorite of German leader Adolf Hitler. Hitler believed

A group of American soldiers shows off a captured Nazi flag.

American General George S. Patton.

that the Allies would be invading far to the north. For weeks flamboyant American General Patton had been seen around Dover, England. Hitler believed that Patton was preparing to lead the invasion from Dover and ignored Rommel's advice.

In fact, General Eisenhower had ordered Patton to Dover in order to trick Hitler. Patton was to draw Hitler's attention to Dover while the real invasion took place at Normandy to the south. Rommel's defenses were weakened by Hitler's error and the Germans could not stop the invasion on the first day. Hitler blamed Rommel for the success of the Allied invasion at Normandy. Later in the war, Hitler accused Rommel of treason and forced him to commit suicide.

As Rommel had predicted, Germany's defeat on "the longest day" led to its defeat in the war. After Generals Bradley and Montgomery oversaw the first phase of the "D-Day" invasion, General Patton was ordered to France to help. Eisenhower made clear, however, that Patton was under the command of Bradley. Under Bradley's direction, the two great generals, Patton and Montgomery, were forced finally to cooperate. Bradley's army defeated the final German attack in January 1945 at the Battle of the Bulge.

In March 1945 the British and American armies crossed the Rhine River into Germany. After Hitler committed suicide on April 30, 1945, German General Alfred Jodl surrendered to the Allies on May 8, 1945, and General Krebs surrendered Berlin to Russian Marshal Georgi Zhukov. Germany was defeated.

The largest battles in World War II took place in Europe and in Africa. It was in Europe and in Africa that the war's most famous generals earned their reputations. The greatest battles in Asia, on the other side of the world, were naval battles fought between ships at sea. Most heroes were sea captains, not army generals.

Nonetheless, General Douglas MacArthur became very famous as the commander of American ground troops against the Japanese. The Japanese surprised MacArthur's troops in the Philippines just as they had surprised the U.S. Navy in the attack on Pearl Harbor on December 7, 1941. MacArthur was forced to flee for his life while thousands of his troops stayed behind in the Philippines to be captured by the Japanese.

Japanese General Masaharu Homma treated his American prisoners with scandalous cruelty, murdering hundreds outright and allowing countless others to die of torture, starvation, and thirst.

Deeply saddened, MacArthur delivered a famous speech in which he promised those left behind that he would return to liberate them soon.

It took several years for MacArthur to organize the liberation. Finally, however, in the spring of 1945, MacArthur returned. One of MacArthur's primary goals was to free the American prisoners before their Japanese guards killed them all.

Although much smaller than the massive battles in Europe, the battles on the Philippine Islands in the South Pacific Ocean were very cruel. The Japanese soldiers now saw that they were losing the war. They fought bitterly in their desperation and were not afraid to die, as long as they could take many American soldiers with them. In the end, however, it was the Japanese who suffered most. Five Japanese soldiers were killed for every American.

General MacArthur became famous for his leadership during the battle of the Philippines. He was rewarded with the honor of accepting the formal Japanese surrender on September 2, 1945.

American General Douglas MacArthur.

General MacArthur signs the Japanese surrender papers aboard the battleship *Missouri*.

World War II was the largest war in history. The great battles were by far the largest the world had ever seen. Successful generals in World War II needed to be more than simple soldiers. They needed to speak and understand foreign languages. They needed to work well with other Allied leaders.

Men like Generals Patton, Alexander, and MacArthur were excellent soldiers, but Generals Eisenhower and Bradley were more successful because they worked better with the Allies. Bradley became the top commander of the American army after the war, while Eisenhower went on to become the 34th president of the United States.

┃NTERNET SITES

A-Bomb WWW Museum
http://www.csi.ad.jp/ABOMB/index.html
    This site provides readers with accurate information concerning the impact of the first atomic bomb on Hiroshima, Japan.

Black Pilots Shatter Myths
http://www.af.mil/news/features/features95/f_950216-112_95feb16.html
    This site tells of the exploits of the 332nd Fighter Group, the first all-black flying unit known as the Tuskegee Airmen.

United States Holocaust Museum
http://www.ushmm.org/
    The official Web site of the U.S. Holocaust Memorial Museum in Washington, D.C.

What Did You Do In The War, Grandma?
http://www.stg.brown.edu/projects/WWII_Women/tocCS.html
    An oral history of Rhode Island women during World War II. In this project, 17 students interviewed 36 Rhode Island women who recalled their lives in the years before, during, and after the Second World War.

World War II Commemoration
http://gi.grolier.com/wwii/wwii_mainpage.html
    To commemorate the 50th anniversary of the end of the war, Grolier Online assembled a terrific collection of World War II historical materials on the Web. Articles taken from *Encyclopedia Americana* tell the story of World War II, including biographies. Also included are combat films, photographs, a World War II history test, and links to many other sites.

These sites are subject to change. Go to your favorite search engine and type in "World War II" for more sites.

Pass It On
    World War II buffs: educate readers around the country by passing on information you've learned about World War II. Share your little-known facts and interesting stories. We want to hear from you! To get posted on the ABDO & Daughters website, E-mail us at "History@abdopub.com"

Visit the ABDO & Daughters website at www.abdopub.com

 29

Blitzkrieg: German word meaning "lightning warfare." Describes a new German military strategy in World War II. *Blitzkrieg* called for very large invasions to overwhelm the enemy quickly and avoid long, drawn out battles.

Churchill, Winston: Prime minister of Great Britain during World War II. He was very famous for his patriotic speeches and fierce resistance to the Germans.

D-Day, June 6, 1944: Code name for the beginning of the great Allied attack on German forces in France.

 Hiroshima: Name of the Japanese city where the United States dropped the first atomic bomb, on August 6, 1945. The city was destroyed.

Maginot Line: Named after the French general who invented the idea, the Maginot Line was a long line of fortresses along the border between France and Germany. It was considered to be absolutely safe and secure. In May 1940 German tanks simply went around the line, through the Ardennes Forest to the north. The Maginot Line proved to be one of the largest military failures in history.

Miracle of Dunkirk: The British navy rescued nearly one million trapped soldiers from certain capture in northern France during May 1940.

Roosevelt, Franklin: President of the U.S. during World War II.

Stuka: A type of German dive bomber. They were very frightening to people because they were so loud and because the Germans had so many of them. They worked to frighten people into submission.

V-E Day, May 8, 1945: After German leader Adolf Hitler committed suicide, the German generals surrendered on May 7. The United States proclaimed May 8 to be "V-E Day," which stood for "Victory in Europe."

Two young victims of war in Naples, Italy.

INDEX

A
Alexander, General Sir Harold 15, 17, 28
Allies 5, 17, 23, 25, 28
Ardennes Forest 7, 8, 9
Asia 26
Auchinleck, General Claude 14, 15
Axis Powers 4, 5

B
Battle of the Bulge 25
Belgium 9
Berlin, Germany 21, 25
Blitzkrieg 6, 7, 8
Bock, General Fedor von 6
Bradley, General Omar 17, 22, 23, 25, 28

C
Chuikov, General Vassily 20
Cunningham, Admiral John 16

D
D-Day 23, 25
Denmark 7
Dover, England 25
Dunkirk, France 9, 10

E
Egypt 10, 12, 14
Eisenhower, General Dwight D. "Ike" 16, 17, 22, 25, 28
El Alamein, Egypt 14, 15, 23
Eremenko, General Andrei 20

F
France 4, 7, 8, 9, 10, 22, 23, 25

G
German Fourth Army 12
Germany 4-7, 10, 12, 13, 20, 21, 23, 25
Great Britain 4, 5, 9, 10, 14
Guderian, General Heinz 8, 9, 10

H
Hitler, Adolf 4-10, 12-15, 23, 25
Homma, General Masaharu 26

I
Italy 4, 17, 20

J
Japan 4, 5, 26, 27
Jodl, General Alfred 25

K
Kasserine Pass, Tunisia 16, 17
Krebs, General 25
Kursk, Soviet Union 21

L
Libya 14

M
MacArthur, General Douglas 26, 27, 28
Maginot, General 7
Maginot Line 7, 8, 9
Montgomery, Field Marshal Sir Bernard 15, 16, 17, 22, 23, 25

N
Normandy, France 23, 25
North Africa 10, 12, 14, 17, 22
Norway 7

O
Operation Torch 16

P
Patton, General George S. 17, 22, 25, 28
Paulus, Field Marshal Friedrich von 12, 13, 20
Pearl Harbor, Hawaii 4, 26
Philippines 26, 27
Poland 4, 6, 7, 8

R
Rhine River, Germany 25
Rokassovsky, General Constantine 21
Rommel, Field Marshal Erwin 8-10, 12, 14-16, 23, 25
Runstedt, General Gerd von 6

S
Sahara Desert 12, 16
Soviet Union 4, 5, 12, 13, 20
Stalin, Josef 20, 21
Stalingrad 12, 13, 20
Stumme, General 15
Switzerland 7

T
Tobruk 14

U
United States 4, 5, 28

W
Wavell, Sir Archibald 14

Z
Zhukov, Marshal Georgi 21, 25